Biblical Gnosis: A Scientific Perspective on the Soul's Ascent

ISBN: 978-0-9906061-7-8

Proudly Published by The Book Shed

By Christian Gnosis

Contact Information

gnosischristian@gmail.com

Modern science and spiritual teachings, especially the Bible, indicate that the human body is a transcendent vessel for the soul.

The cerebral cortex is the part of the brain that generates higher cognitive processing and your ability to perceive your self, or simply referred to as your ego. The cortex is arranged into various compartments. At the center is the central sulcus, which is the functional midline of the brain. This midline is represented as the present moment. The central sulcus is the neuroanatomical substrate of the present moment; the now. The frontal lobe is in front of this midline; this can be represented as the future. This is because the frontal lobe involves all planning on what you "will do", "what is going to be done", "what to expect", or anything involving future matters. As you get closer to the midline, the intended action becomes closer to the present, for example, the far front is responsible for complex, somewhat abstract plans, and when you approach the midline this becomes the part of the brain that actually controls your limbs to do the planned action. So, if you think, "Wave at your brother", the initial idea comes to your mind in the frontal association areas, whereas the actual initiation of your arm and shoulder muscles to execute the wave happens at the primary motor cortex adjacent to the central sulcus.

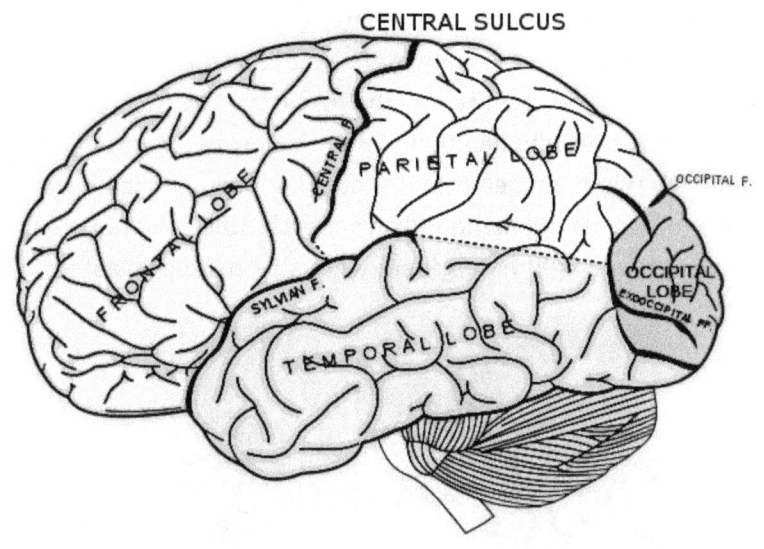

The same is true for the area behind the midline, the parietal lobe. This is sensory perception. All sensory perception, by the time it actually reaches your cognizant self, is an artifact of the past, you are "feeling" something that actually "happened" milliseconds ago.

There is a brain segment that transcends, or passes over this midline, this is the temporal lobe. This section is most notably responsible for memory; something that requires an integration of past feelings, and future plans to generate a concept of what we call time. The temporal lobe extends across the present midline, incorporating the past future and present into its function.

There is another line that cross-roads with the central sulcus, the longitudinal fissure. This divides the left and right hemispheres. The right hemisphere functions as a holistic, macroscopic sort of machine, it understands the whole picture more so than its constituent parts. The left hemisphere is a logical, microscopic sort of machine, it understands the constituent parts more so than the whole picture. This dichotomy was epitomized by the research of Dr. Gazzaniga. Using someone who had their corpus callosum cut, meaning the patient's two brain hemispheres could not communicate and therefore acted independently from each other, the functions of the left and right hemisphere were able to be elucidated.

His right hemisphere saw this image of a man assembled from vegetables as a man, whereas his left hemisphere saw this picture as a bunch of vegetables. The left hemisphere was incapable of understanding the whole, but rather defined the object as its constituent parts. The right hemisphere understood the whole, and was able to identify this picture as a representation of a man. The right hemisphere uses a macroscopic perspective whereas the left hemisphere uses a microscopic perspective.

The left brain hemisphere is in control of the right hand, whereas the right brain hemisphere controls the left hand. This is not a type, each brain hemisphere controls the opposite side of the body. This gives us clues as to our current psyche as a species. Our population is 90% right-handed. This is a testament to our left-brain dominant society (remember the left brain controls right side of body). We have forgotten the whole, the big picture, and rather microscoped our beliefs into a theory based purely off logic; otherwise known as science. Science, Darwin, etc, is essentially the religion of our age. We take science to be the dogma of what *is* in the world. I am not saying science is incorrect. it is important. Or rather, half of the puzzle to life.

The right-brained, or left-handed, viewpoint was once the dominant way of understanding the world. This was a holistic viewpoint which lacked a lot of left-brained, scientific support. The ancients had a general intuitive idea of what *is*, but did not necessarily have logical evidence to support their notions. This is exemplified in all holy, or sacred texts. They were intuitive, holistic accounts of what *is*. This notion is further supported by the fact that ancient texts were written from right to left, implicating the usage of the left hand. A society with mostly left handed people indicates a dominant right brained ideology. Hebrew, Aramaic, Arabic, etc, the languages in which many holy texts were originally written, have a right to left written language. A right to left written language is designed for the left hand. On the contrary, a left to right written language, such as English, is designed for a population that is mostly right handed.

A comprehensive understanding of both spirituality and

science, a union of both left and right brained thinking, are required to gain a complete understanding of the world and unlock its great secrets. Just as you do not want to be enthralled with the past or present, you do not want to be caught up in microscopic or macroscopic thinking, but rather a balance of both. Coordinating spirit and science, right and left brain, is the key to understanding. Post-mortem studies of Albert Einstein's brain indicated that he had an amazingly thick corpus callosum; implying that the connections and communication between his left and right brain were numerous.

The pineal gland is centrally located in the brain in between the two hemispheres and between the frontal and parietal lobes. Within the crevasse of the midline, which represents the present, a balance of left and right brained thinking, resides the pineal gland. Renee Descartes claimed it to be the seat of the soul, and he appears to be quite accurate. This is where "You" are, or should be. It is important to orient yourself at the present moment in order to avoid the anxiety that coincides with orienting yourself in the past or future. The best way to actively engulf yourself in the present is to focus on your breathing. Your breathing is always synched with the present moment. Focusing on your breath is a great natural analgesic, or pain reliever. By focusing on your breath, your consciousness disregards the pain and connects you with the present moment, rather than milliseconds in the "past" where the sensation of pain resides. This worked perfectly for me when I used to get migraine headaches.

Furthermore, your anxieties manifest as physical compulsions. Whether it be Tourette's syndrome or simply cracking your knuckles, your anxiety initiates unnecessary action in your cerebral cortex. This excessive activity in your brain is stress. All stress comes from disorienting yourself from the present, and entrancing yourself with the past or future. If you are feeling stress or anxiety, focus on your breath and your anxiety will dissolve. If you notice yourself cracking your knuckles, biting your nails, etc, this is your cue that you are anxious: when this happens allocate your focus to your breath. Take solace in the present, it is a gift. The past and future are not actually real, they are just a creation of your brain. All that is, and ever will be, Is right now. Think about what happens when you put two mirrors facing each other and stand in between. You see an endless number of reflections within the mirrors. This simple experiment demonstrates the infinitude of the present moment.

"In eternity there is indeed something true and sublime. But all these times and places and occasions are now and here. God himself culminates in the present moment, and will never be more divine in the lapse of all the ages. And we are enabled to apprehend at all what is sublime and noble only by the perpetual instilling and drenching of the reality that surrounds us."

Henry David Thoreau, *Walden*

Nikola Tesla, master of alternating current among many other things, knew of the powers of the brain. Nikola Tesla designed a tower "As a means for transmitting electrical energy to a distance through the natural media (air)..." [1]. This tower is essentially a replica of the human brain, and its purpose is to transmit power wirelessly. From the spinal cord, to the cerebral cortex, Tesla's wireless transmission device is a reproduction of the neuronal system of a human. He even discusses how the tower bulb should have dimples and divots, just like the cerebral cortex. This tower was actually constructed. During the world war it was torn down because the military feared that the enemy could use it for espionage purposes. This structure is also seen in the Tesla coil. If a structure designed from the human neuronal system can transmit power wirelessly, does this mean the same for the human brain?

Many experiments have been conducted that demonstrate some sort of connection with humanity and nature. For example, as demonstrated in the movie *I Am*, a strain of microorganisms was hooked up to a voltmeter. A man, physically unattached to the microorganisms, was told to think of something stressful. Upon thinking of his divorce, the voltmeter spiked right on cue with the man's stressful thought. It is as if the microorganisms felt the man's anxiety and responded with a phenomenal spike in voltage. How could this be possible?

In the bones of our nose are fragments of ferrous oxide (magnetite) which respond to electromagnetic impulses. This, among other neuroanatomical substrates, may be serving as a sort of antenna for each human to be connected to the collective. Research discussed by Robert O. Becker in the Body Electric demonstrated that electromagnetic waves have a magnificent impact on the human. Two underground rooms were created without any clocks or windows to the outside world. The only difference between the two underground rooms was that one was made to be void of external electromagnetic influence whereas the other was left with normal electromagnetic fields from the earth, sun, moon, etc. The group with electromagnetic influence was amazingly able to maintain a consistent circadian rhythm without being able to see the normal light/dark cycles of the sun, but the group without electromagnetic influence became erratic and their circadian rhythms were significantly disrupted. There are countless other experiments that prove a vital relationship between humans and electromagnetism, buy I will not flood you with detail from other experiments.

Robert Becker also incidentally identified the physical basis for the 7 chakras of Hindu and yogic tradition. The chakras are energy centers aligned along the brain and spine. Robert Becker found the scientific substrate for these 7 chakras that have been known by mystics and the spiritually adept for millennia. In the spine there are two enlargements (shown as + along the spine in the picture); the cervical enlargement is attributed to the mass of neuronal cell bodies that project to your arms, the lumbar enlargement is a similar mass of neuronal cell bodies that projects to your legs. These enlargements house a significant positive charge in relation to the rest of the spine. These two areas are literally charged, just like the mystics proposed with the chakras. The cervical enlargement anatomically matches the location of the throat chakra, and the lumbar enlargement anatomically matches the location of the solar plexus chakra. At the midpoint between these two locations of the spine is the sinoatrial node of the heart.

The sinoatrial node is an independent mass of neuronal bodies that maintains a necessary pace for heart. Although the heart itself is oblique and off-centered, the sinoatrial node is located at the central axis of the spine, in vertical alignment with the cervical and lumbar enlargement. The curvature of the spine allows the sinoatrial node to vertically align with the two

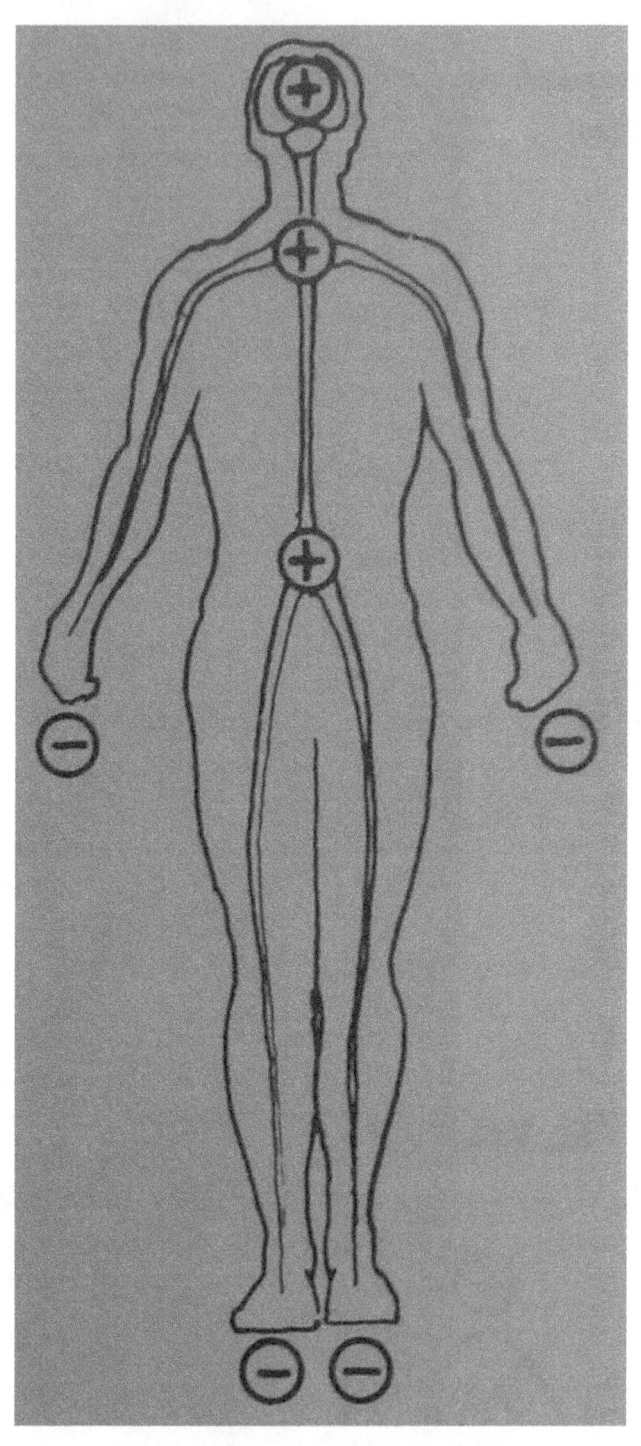

enlargements. Becker also found another location of significant positive charge, the cerebral cortex. He found that this positive charge encapsulates the brain, and this is the electrophysiological basis for the crown chakra. In between the crown chakra and the cervical enlargement, aligned in perfect vertical orientation, is the pineal gland. The 3rd eye chakra. The physical substrate which acts as an internal gateway to the spiritual realm.

The pineal gland is responsible for "The mediation of spontaneous mystical and visionary states..." [2] and is also what establishes a regular circadian rhythm by a cyclic release of melatonin among other hormones. I'm sure you have heard of DMT, if not I would suggest learning about it. DMT is made in the pineal gland [3] and its release is the current explanation for the visualizations that concur with a near death experience. DMT has a chemical analog that can be found in high concentrations in certain species of fungi; psilocybes. Psilocybin, found in "magic mushrooms", gets metabolized in the body to

DMT

Psilocin

psilocin. You may have a negative presupposition regarding the magic mushroom. I encourage you to reconsider. Nature is a Divine creation, and the magic mushroom is here to help us.

Psilocin and DMT are nearly identical, and thus create

similar reactions in the brain. Let's go into greater detail about the mysterious mushroom. But I want to quickly note that DMT is the natural way in which your body can experience the spiritual world, hence its name as the spirit molecule. DMT can be thought of as the chemical neurotransmitter of spirit which intensifies with a properly functioning pineal gland. Psilocin, of magic mushrooms, is a way to artificially simulate this process and give you a glimpse into the spiritual world. Eating psilocybin mushrooms instills:

"Changes in the perception of the **ego** and the self; feelings of unification with nature and universe, peak experiences, nirvana, ecstasy, rapture, extreme euphoria, excitement and happiness, oceanic bliss, self-fulfillment" [4].

These mushrooms were deified by aboriginal cultures such as the Native Americans because taking magic mushrooms allowed you to participate in the Divine. In 'The Sacred Mushroom & The Cross' by John Allegro, Christianity is discussed in relation to the mindset that occurs during a trip on mushrooms. Magic mushrooms are like a spiritual propellant into the Christ mind. So, what does scientific report tell us is going on during a mushroom trip?

Psilocin silences the cerebral cortex, the part of the brain that generates the ego. This allows more primitive brain regions to increase their expression. Now this may sound like a stupefying effect, if it is to silence more "advanced" regions of the brain. But, the cerebral cortex is what generates the ego, the feeling of separateness from the All. Dr Robin Carhart-Harris, a post-doctoral researcher in neuropsychopharmacology, explains that magic mushroom users are essentially feeling a temporary silencing of the ego. With a death to the ego, one is able to see the coordinated nature of the universe and feel intense spiritual integration. With our egoic barriers temporarily dismantled, we are able to feel a synchrony with the external world. A realization that our being is connected to the Divine Mind. A death to the ego allows the body to integrate into the higher power that is.

    A wonderful example of someone who experienced such an ego-death, via the silencing of the cerebral cortex, is Dr. Eben Alexander. Dr. Alexander was a typical skeptic of spirituality prior to a bout with meningitis. Meningitis put him into a deep coma in which his "...entire neocortex (cerebral cortex) – the outer surface of the brain, the part that makes us human – was entirely shut down, inoperative..." During his coma-like state, NY Times reports that:

    "During that week, as life slipped away, he now says, he was living intensely in his mind. He was reborn into a primitive mucky Jell-o-like substance and then guided by "a beautiful girl with high cheekbones and deep blue eyes" on the wings of a butterfly to an "immense void" that is both "pitch black" and "brimming with light" coming from an "orb" that interprets for an all-loving God."

    Dr. Alexander was so compelled by his visions that he wrote a book called "Proof of Heaven". When his cerebral cortex was shut down, he was able to connect to the Divine. We must tame our cerebral cortex, that is, our ego. In Alchemical lore, this is called taming the beast. We must tame our egotistical desires, and use our cerebral cortex for creating Good and fulfilling our purpose like it was meant to do.

    Along with silencing the ego, psilocin also silences all the brain waves generated by your brain except for a certain frequency of waves. Gamma waves, not to be confused with gamma rays, are the highest frequency brain wave emitted by the human brain. These gamma waves are the only set of waves not inhibited by psilocin[5]. Therefore, you are left with nothing but an abundance of this high frequency gamma waveform generated from your brain. Gamma waves have been correlated with expanded consciousness, spiritual revelation, and a feeling of love. Be cautious though, because a dissolved ego can result in a manic episode if you are not ready for it. Many have been blinded by the light, figuratively speaking. If you plan on consuming mushrooms make sure the time and setting are right. Usually it is best to be in nature. I am also not saying we should all just be on mushrooms all the time, it is just a way for you to get a glimpse into the higher realm.

"Psychedelic experience is only a glimpse of genuine mystical insight, but a glimpse which can be matured and deepened by the various ways of meditation in which drugs are no longer necessary or useful. If you get the message, hang up the phone. For psychedelic drugs are simply instruments, like microscopes, telescopes, and telephones. The biologist does not sit with eye permanently glued to the microscope, he goes away and works on what he has seen."

-Alan Watts

Watts is spot on here, this feeling can be achieved naturally. Gamma wave activity, the natural brain wave that is correlated with such an elevated consciousness, was shown to increase considerably during meditation [6], especially when the meditator thought of "unconditional loving-kindness and compassion" [7]. Unconditional love is a natural way to silence your ego and feel your presence in the All. Gamma waves are an indication of an elevated state of being, and they are triggered by love. All those who have professed the power of love were right, it is literally empowering, puts a death to the ego, and integrates our being with the All. Many of you may disassociate Darwin with the notions that I have been discussing, and would rather relate Darwin with "survival of the fittest". This is, to an extent, a misconception. Here in the concluding words in the descent of man:

"Important as the struggle for existence has been and even still is, yet as far as the highest part of our nature is concerned there are other agencies more important. For the moral qualities are advanced either directly or indirectly much more through the effects of habit, by our reasoning powers, by instruction, by religion, etc., than through natural selection.... But the more important elements for us are love, and the distinct emotion of sympathy.... The birth both of the species and of the individual are equally parts of that grand sequence of events that our minds refuse to accept as the result of blind chance. The understanding revolts at such a conclusion."

Furthermore, Darwin mentions survival of the fittest only twice in the descent of man, whereas he mentions love 95 times.

Among many other prophetic figures, Jesus preached love and selflessness , or ego-lessness, and faith in a higher power. He claimed that by doing this you would enter into God's kingdom. Heaven is commonly assumed to be a place where good people go when they die. Yet, the bible makes no claims that heaven is obtainable only after death. In fact, it is quite the opposite. The bible eludes to The Kingdom of Heaven as a gift to the righteous living on earth.

    I want to present a quick prelude before I start quoting biblical passages. I understand many of you may have resentment for organized religion, and this may have alienated you from faith in general. If you haven't already, I insist you give it another chance, with an open mind, and try to understand it on your own. Furthermore, I am also going to quote gnostic gospels. These are gospels which are not considered by many organized Christian sects to be the word of God. You will see that the messages in these gospels are similar to the Orthodox gospels. Regardless, my presentation does not rely on these passages, but rather uses them as a supplement of understanding. I suggest that you at least consider these gospels as Divinely Inspired. I am going to present my interpretation and I hope it helps your own understanding. Some of you may be shaking your head, and I am aware that atheist ideology has become rampant in our world. An atheist is like a blind man claiming that colors do not exist. An atheist could argue this by saying that a believer is like a blind man who claims he knows what colors are. This is partly why Jesus came to earth; he came to give sight to the spiritually blind.

    Jesus Christ was sent to the world to save humanity. Save humankind from what? Plato, the great Greek philosopher, presents a parable. "The Allegory of The Cave", written around 380 BC, describes how we as humans are trapped in an illusion. The movie "The Matrix" is based off this allegory. This allegory describes prisoners, enslaved by their own ignorance, living in a cave in which their reality consists of shadows. They are ignorant to the fact that there is a deeper reality to these shadows. Upon understanding and practicing philosophy, they begin to discern between reality and illusion. As knowledge is obtained and practiced, they begin to see the light coming from outside and begin their ascent out of the cave; realizing that the shadows were only a vestige of the true reality. At first, the light, the true reality, outside the cave is overwhelming. The prisoner will be initially blinded by the light. But, eventually their eyes adjust and are able to approach the more real existence. Plato says we are like the prisoners and "...the journey upwards (is) the ascent of the soul into the intellectual world."

"Enter through the narrow gate. For wide is the gate and broad is the road that leads to destruction, and many enter through it. But small is the gate and narrow the road that leads to life, and only a few find it" (Matthew 7:13).

The Path to paradise is thought to be razor thin, requiring extensive discipline. Jesus Christ is considered to be the archetype of The Path; "(Jesus) left you an example so that you could follow in his footsteps" (1 Peter 2:21). Jesus can be considered in the Cave Allegory as a philosopher coming from outside the cave to teach the prisoners about their plight and help them escape. In the allegory, Plato explains that if someone were to return after ascending out of the cave, the prisoners—the unenlightened—would ridicule what the returning person would have to say. Upon hearing the great philosopher who came from the light, the prisoners would think that "...he came without his eyes; and that it was better not even to think of ascending; and if any one tried to loose another and lead him up to the light, **let them only catch the offender, and they would put him to death.**" Hundreds of years later, Jesus, the Son of God sent to teach the earth about The Kingdom of God, was captured and crucified. Plato's clairvoyance here is amazing. He successfully predicted the coming life of Christ. The world of imperfection in which we currently live is the cave, The Kingdom of God awaits outside the cave, and The Path is the process of ascension out of the cave.

So, how did the human descend into the cave? The story of Genesis explains how Adam and Eve were placed in paradise and "…were created in (God's) image" (Genesis 1:27). Upon finishing creation "God saw all that he had made, and it was very good" (Genesis 1:31). Similarly, in Plato's Timaeus, a demiurge is described who creates the world as a copy of the eternal, unchanging Divine Image. This creation is teleological in nature; the universe is arranged in a certain way to yield good results out of chaos. This is an interesting point. Science has demonstrated that the entropy, or randomness, of the universe is constantly increasing. Despite this fact, the human body is immensely complex and organized. If randomness is always increasing in the universe, how could elaborate organization, such as the human being, assimilate? This order, amongst chaos, is Divine craftsmanship. After He created humanity in His Image, God warned "…you must not eat from the tree of the knowledge of good and evil, for when you eat from it you will certainly die" (Genesis 2:17). When you sin, you diverge yourself from the Image of God. The Image of God will be discussed later, for now let's examine what sin is.

Sin, in Greek, means to "miss the mark": a deviation from Divine purpose. The bible repeatedly explains the penalty for sin:

"For the wages of sin is death, but the gift of God is eternal life in Christ Jesus our Lord" (Romans 6:23).

"Truly the righteous attain life, but whoever pursues

evil finds death" (Proverbs 11:19).

"The one who sins is the one who will die" (Ezekiel 18:4).

"(sinners) will go away into eternal punishment, but the righteous into eternal life" (Matthew 25:45).

"Therefore, just as sin entered the world through one man, and death through sin, and in this way death came to all people, because all sinned..." (Romans 5:12).

The 7 deadly sins are literally deadly.

The Old Testament elucidates certain types of sin which occur on a societal scale. The agricultural revolution was a pivotal shift in human thinking. For example, the agricultural revolution led to the foundation and rise of civilization. In order to prevent the construction of a city the people planned to build, God scrambled their language at the tower, or "city" (Genesis 11:4), of Babel. The health disparities that arose from the agricultural revolution are explained by Jared Diamond in 'The Worst Mistake in the History of the Human Race" published in Discovery Magazine. But, the main concern is the collective ego of the people ruling the given city. This is epitomized in the story of Moses' exodus out of Egypt. Pharaoh's despotic rule is typical of civilization throughout history. There are countless documentaries that demonstrate this rabid power structure and how it effects our world today. Imperialism has been strangling the livelihood of the world for millennia. This power, rooted in ravenous egotistic endeavors, has been present since the fall of mankind. Like prisoners in Plato's Cave Allegory, we are all subject to such tyranny. The story of Exodus is exemplifying an escape from mental slavery and a movement towards the Promised Land; just like Plato's

Cave. The Pharaoh represents the ego, impeding The Path to salvation. Society and the status quo is strangling your spiritual progress:

> "Do not conform to the pattern of this world, but be transformed by the renewing of your mind. Then you will be able to test and approve what God's will is – his good, pleasing and perfect will."
>
> (Romans 12:2)

Society is the great illusion that people consider to be the "real" world. We are all told as children that we must grow up and get a job. Death and taxes are the only certainties that we were raised to believe. This is the opposite of our spiritual destiny. We have a choice in the matter. Death and taxes, or eternal life and liberty. This is exemplified by Jesus' disciples dropping their nets (quitting their jobs as fisherman) and following Jesus to a new life (Matthew 4:18-20). Jesus explains that we must leave our old life, the life of materialism. Upon doing this we begin our spiritual ascent:

Just then a man came up to Jesus and asked, "Teacher, what good thing must I do to get eternal life?"

Jesus answered, "If you want to be perfect, go, sell your possessions and give to the poor, and you will have treasure in heaven. Then come, follow me."

When the young man heard this, he went away sad, because he had great wealth.

Then Jesus said to his disciples, "Truly I tell you, it is hard for someone who is rich to enter the kingdom of heaven. [24] Again I tell you, it is easier for a camel to go through the eye of a needle than for someone who is rich to enter the kingdom of God."

When the disciples heard this, they were greatly astonished and asked, "Who then can be saved?"

Jesus looked at them and said, "With man this is impossible, but with God all things are possible."

Peter answered him, "We have left everything to follow you! What then will there be for us?"

Jesus said to them, "Truly I tell you, at the renewal of all things, when the Son of Man sits on his glorious throne, you who have followed me will also sit on twelve thrones, judging the twelve tribes of Israel. And everyone who has left houses or brothers or sisters or father or mother or wife or children or fields for my sake will receive a hundred times as much and will inherit eternal life.

(Matthew 19: 16, 21-29)

Similarly, there is a Zen proverb in which a man leaves his material life and goes off into the wilderness and is never heard from again. The ego attaches the person to the material world and prevents spiritual progress:

"Matter gave birth to a passion that has no equal, which proceeded from something contrary to nature. Then there arises a disturbance in its whole body."

(Mary Magdalene Chapter 4 Line 30)

"Whoever sows to please their flesh, from the flesh will reap destruction; whoever sows to please the Spirit, from the Spirit will reap eternal life."   (Galatians 6:8)

"Through the abandonment of desire, the deathless state is realized."

(Buddhism: Samyatta Nikaya xlvii 37)

So, where is the Kingdom of God? Do not expect the Hubble telescope to one day find a man with a long gray beard residing in a distant galaxy. Rather, the Divine energy, God, is within you, eager to be awakened.

"Neither shall they say, Lo here! Or, lo there! For, behold, the kingdom of God is within you" (Luke 17:21)

This is similar to the Eastern philosophy of "Atman is Brahman". Atman is the avatar, or your individual consciousness. Brahman is the entire external world. All is One, and One is All. You are not an insignificant one in 7 billion, but rather you are one whose internal state influences the world on a mass scale. People wonder why the world is so imperfect, but they are blind to their own imperfections which are manifesting on a local and global scale. This is why Jesus is so disgusted with hypocrites; they preach righteousness but act unrighteously. "Woe to you, teachers of the law and Pharisees, you hypocrites! You clean the outside of the cup and dish, but inside they are full of greed and self-indulgence" (Matthew 23:23). Like someone who puts a "Stop the fracking" bumper sticker on their gas-powered automobile.

"Why do you look at the speck of sawdust in your brother's eye and pay no attention to the plank in your own eye? How can you say to your brother, 'Let me take the speck out of your eye,' when all the time there is a plank in your own eye? You hypocrite, first take the plank out of your own eye, and then you will see clearly to remove the speck from your brother's eye."   (Matthew 7:3-5)

To quote Mahatma Ghandi, "You must be the change you wish to see in the world." Upon solving your inner conflict, the world will follow suite. Trying to directly change the outer world, without changing yourself, is futile.

"Why do you wash the outside of the cup? Don't you understand that the one who made the inside is also the one who made the outside?" (Thomas 89).

"...There is light within a person of light, and it shines on the whole world. If it does not shine, it is dark." (Thomas 24).

Or simply, you reap what you sow. Karma. Many criticize God's actions in the Old Testament as malevolent, and outright absurd. But, God is the enforcer, or embodiment, of karmic Judgment.

"God is the Rock, his works are perfect, and all his ways are just. A faithful God who does no wrong, upright and just he is" (Deuteronomy 32:4).

"And the heavens proclaim his righteousness, for he is a God of justice" (Psalm 50:6).

People get what they deserve. "...every good tree bears good fruit, but a bad tree bears bad fruit" (Matthew 7:17). The authors of the Old Testament were cognizant of this karmic Law and they referred to it as God. When Moses asked God who he was, God responded "I am that I am" (Exodus 3:14). God Is that "I Am" factor, that Being within all of us. This "I Am-ness" is the Son of Man referred to in the bible. The Son of Man, literally meaning that which is spawned from man, is the I Am. The unity we hold with The One, The Being, The All. Jesus exemplified what man could do, and expressed the word of God so that we too could live the life of Christ and integrate into heaven. The Son of Man is what is "lifted up" into heaven: "No one has ever gone into heaven except the one who came from heaven—the Son of Man" (John 3:13). The Son of Man and the Kingdom of Heaven are within all of us, waiting to be unlocked. With the proper understanding of what the Son of Man is, certain bible passages make much more sense:

So Jesus Said, "When you have lifted up the Son of Man, then you will know that I am he and that I do nothing on my own but speak just what the Father has taught me" (John 8:28)

Upon confusion of the parable of the seed Jesus answered "The one who sowed the good seed is the Son of Man. The field and the good seed stands for the people of the kingdom" (Matthew 13:37-38).

"Truly I tell you, some who are standing here will not taste death before they see the Son of Man entering his kingdom" (Matthew 16:28).

The Son of Man is described in the Metaphysical Bible Dictionary by Charles Fillmore:

"Jesus represents God's idea of man in expression (Son of Man); Christ is that idea in the absolute. The Christ is the man that God created in His image and likeness, the perfect-idea man, and is the real self of all men. The son of man is the thought of this spiritual man, or idea of God, and like all thoughts is subject to the limitations of its own identity. By voluntarily casting off these limitations the man identity may come into realization of its own universality as the only begotten of God. So we find Jesus referring to Himself as both the "Son of God" and the "Son of Man", because He had reached a place in understanding where He realized His relation to Being."

The Son of Man can be thought of as a butterfly, whereas our current state is the caterpillar. We are destined to one day be born into something new. Just like the butterfly is the born-again creation of the caterpillar, the Son of Man is the born-again creation of the human. Jesus exemplified the power of the Son of Man. He often referred to himself as the Son of Man because he was not merely human, but rather the unleashed potential that can be birthed by the human. The "one who sowed the good seed". The Son of Man is revealed internally by relinquishing evil ways, a death to the ego, love, and faith in your new understanding. By doing this your brain readjusts to its primordial state, which allows it to transmit Divine Thought. This experience is artificially simulated by the magic mushroom. Transmission of Divine Thought is clouded by sin. Sin is like a virus in our brain that causes it to dysfunction.

Satan may not actually be a tangible entity, but rather a culmination of everyone's sin. Satan can also be simplified as the ego. Once Satan is driven out, through purification and ego removal, the kingdom of God is presented internally and externally with faith. This underworld we are living in is "ruled" by Satan. We enslave ourselves, through defying Divine law, and manifest a world of imperfection and death. "but, the evil's upon the earth, **which men create**, are inspired by that spirit which now worketh in the children of disobedience"

(Ephesians 2:1-2)

Jesus fulfilled his mission so that the Word of God could spread to help people escape this mental slavery and live an eternal spiritual life:

"Since the children have flesh and blood, he too shared in their humanity so that by his death he might break the power of him who holds the power of death — that is, the devil..." (Hebrews 2:14).

"The Last enemy that will be destroyed is death"

(1 Corinthians 15:26).

"but it has now been revealed through the appearing of our Savior, Christ Jesus, who has destroyed death and has brought life and immortality to light through the gospel"

(2 Timothy 1:10).

The Savior said "There is no sin, but it is you who make sin when you do the things that are like the nature of adultery, which is called sin… That is why you become sick and die, for you are deprived of the one who can heal you… Beware that no one lead you astray saying Lo here or lo there! For the **Son of Man** is within you. Follow after Him! Those who seek Him will find Him…"

(Mary Magdelene 4:26, 28, 34-36).

Sin is a neurologic perversion, and this manifests as illness. Sin causes the bodily decay process, due to a lack of Divine sustenance. The human body has all the required tools to repair any abnormality. This is why the mystery of death has eluded scientists. They can't thoroughly explain what causes the body to quit repairing itself. During my Junior year of undergraduate school I took a class on the neuroscience of aging, expecting to get some scientific answers. The answer was, "we have no answer". This is because science ignores spirituality! If they were to analyze spiritual teachings they would see it clear as day. Sin causes death and decay. So, what allows us to heal? Faith.

Jesus turned and saw her. "Take heart, daughter," he said, "your **faith** has healed you." And the woman was healed at that moment

(Matthew 9:22).

When Jesus saw their **faith**, he said to the paralyzed man, "Son, your sins are forgiven" ..."I tell you, get up, take your mat and go home." He got up, took his mat and walked out in full view of them all...

(Mark 2:5, 11-12).

"Go," said Jesus, "your **faith** has healed you." Immediately he received his sight and followed Jesus along the road

(Mark 10:52).

Faithlessness disempowers such healing ability:

"...And (Jesus) did not do many miracles there because of their lack of faith"

(Matthew 13:58).

Remember, the devil holds the power of death (Hebrews 2:14). We have free will, and through choosing sin, we die due to our neurologic perversion. Through faith sins are forgiven:

"When Jesus saw their faith, he said, 'Friend, your sins are forgiven'" (Luke 5:20).

And it is through faith that eternal life is granted:

"For God so loved the world that he gave his one and only Son, that whoever believes in him shall not perish but have eternal life" (John 3:16).

"Because you will not abandon me to the realm of the dead, nor will you let your faithful one see decay"

(Psalms 16:10).

In science, healing through faith has been classified as the placebo effect. The placebo phenomenon describes patients consistently receiving therapeutic benefits from an inert pill. In other words, people are healed by their faith. This is scientific report of healing through faith. On the other hand, faithlessness or pessimism culminates the nocebo effect, which causes a worsened outcome due to a bad mentality. This is fear, or stress, that is causing bodily ailment. Healing is just the beginning for one who integrates, believes, and acts on the philosophy of Christ:

"If you believe, you will receive whatever you ask for in prayer"

(Matthew 21:22).

"Truly I tell you, if you have faith as small as a mustard seed, you can say to this mountain, 'Move from here to there,' and it will move. Nothing will be impossible for you"

(Matthew 17:20).

"Truly I tell you, if anyone says to this mountain 'Go, throw yourself into the sea,' and does not doubt in their heart but believes that what they say will happen, it will be done for them"

(Mark 11:23).

This makes sense of how the patriarchs in Genesis lived so long. Adam lived 930 years, Seth died at 912, Enosh died at 905 years, and so forth (Genesis 5). One might argue that they were likely counting in lunar years, but this is not the case. Mahalalel was 65 when he became the father of Jared (Genesis 5:15). If this were lunar cycles, Mahalalel would have been a 5 year old father.

Even more mysterious is the case of Enoch. He lived a total of 365 years, and instead of dying he "...walked **faithfully** with God; then he was no more, because God took him away"

(Genesis 5:24).

"By faith Enoch was taken up so that he should not see death..."

(Hebrews 11:5).

Similar to Enoch, "...Elijah went up by a whirlwind to heaven" (2 Kings 2:11). These are written accounts of ascension into the spiritual realm. Jesus did the same after he rose from the dead. The bible is essentially a how-to manual on tapping into our Divine nature, but we are all sinning, or "missing the mark", and dying. Eternal life is tough to wrap our heads around. The Jews are befuddled when Jesus claims one can elude death, and Jesus tries to explain this concept:

"I am not possessed by a demon," said Jesus, "but I honor my Father and you dishonor me... Very truly I tell you, whoever obeys my word will never see death."

At this they exclaimed, "Now we know that you are demon-possessed! Abraham died and so did the prophets, yet you say that whoever obeys your word will never taste death. Are you greater than our father Abraham? He died, and so did the prophets. Who do you think you are?"

Jesus replied, "If I glorify myself, my glory means nothing. My Father, whom you claim as your God, is the one who glorifies me. Though you do not know him, I know him... Your father Abraham rejoiced at the thought of seeing my day; he saw it and was glad."

"You are not yet fifty years old," they said to him, "and you have seen Abraham!"

"Very truly I tell you," Jesus answered, "before Abraham was born, **I am**!"

How was Abraham able to see Jesus? Abraham entered into that I Am, the kingdom of Heaven within. This is the Covenant he shared with God. Deification, or integration into the Kingdom of God, is an overlooked theme in the bible, but it is undeniable:

"Jesus answered them, 'Is it not written in your Law, that ye are gods?" (John 10:34)

Here Jesus is referring to Psalm 82:

"You are 'gods'; you are all sons of the Most High..."

Lowercase 'gods' is referring to the fallen state of humankind (our current being), and it is further stated that these gods will die like mere mortals because "The 'gods' know nothing, they understand nothing. They walk about in darkness..." (Psalm 82:5). It is through Divine knowledge and understanding, the philosophical ascent out of Plato's Cave of ignorance, that we begin to reintegrate with the Being that is transcendent of time, God.

"Seeing that His divine power has granted to us everything pertaining to life and godliness, through the true knowledge of Him who called us by His own glory and excellence. For by these He has granted to us His precious and magnificent promises, so that by them you may become partakers of the divine nature, having escaped the corruption that is in the world caused by evil desires. Now for this very reason also, applying all diligence, in your faith supply moral excellence, and in your moral excellence, knowledge..."

(2 Peter 1:3-5)

This is the integration into the kingdom of Heaven. A homecoming that reunites humanity with their Divine origin. This is why the ego, which sins, is so detrimental. A selfish mentality disallows a synchronization with a higher form of being. Remember, meditating, or "praying", with faith and unconditional love allows you to "see" or "feel" God. Or, as Plato says:

"...in the world of knowledge the idea of good appears last of all, and is seen only with an effort; and, when seen, is also inferred to be **the universal author of all things beautiful and right, parent of light and of the lord of light in this visible world, and the immediate source of reason and truth in the intellectual**; and that this is the power upon which he who would act rationally, either in public or private life must have his eye fixed."

This good that we must have our eyes fixed upon is the Divine Image. This is the knowledge that Socrates believes is pre-existent in our memory as explained by his Theory of Recollection. This pre-existent knowledge has also been called the Akashic Records. In neuroscience this is called a phyletic memory; something that is innately programmed into the human. For example, we are all born knowing how to walk, it is just a matter of obtaining the leg strength to be able to support our body weight. Hover an infant over a treadmill, thus supporting his body weight, and the walking motion will be revealed. Similarly, God's Image is present within us from birth. We were made in his image "So God created mankind in his own image, in the image of God he create them; male and female...."

(Genesis 1:27).

This Image, which Plato describes as being an unchanging and eternal form, becomes revealed to us, as Socrates explains in his Theory of Recollection, through philosophical pursuit of the Form highest in the hierarchy; The Good. Greek and Christian thought is referring to the same sort of Divinity here. We are literally the embodiment of Good, as

God's image, but our free will allows us to do evil if we so choose, as demonstrated by Adam and Eve. Then we consciously fell out of paradise and became limited in our abilities and subject to death because we participated in imperfection.

And the Lord God said, "The man has now become like one of us, knowing good and evil. He must not be allowed to reach out his hand and take also from the tree of life and eat, and live forever."

(Genesis 3:22)

They were no longer the embodiment of pure Goodness, but rather participants in evil and thus decay.

When asked to describe the Good, Socrates presents an allegory, and claims it is analogous to the Sun. The luminary at the outside of Plato's cave is the Sun; The Form of the Good, The Divine Image, The Kingdom of Heaven, Light. We are on a journey to reintegrate with the Good, "…the Good came into your midst, to the essence of every nature in order to restore it to its root."

(Mary Magdalene 4:27)

Since this Image is unchanging, eternal, "The Alpha and the Omega" (Revelations 1:8), It is not subject to time. It is a 4th dimensional entity, time itself, whereas we are currently 3rd dimensional entities bound by time. Similar to how our 2nd dimensional shadows are limited by the 3rd dimension, our 3rd dimensional being is currently bound by 4th dimensional time-space. Our wickedness has made us mere shadows of the 4th dimension. The 4th dimension is the Good itself, or light. To complete Plato's analogy, he is implying that our 3rd

dimensional existence is an illusion, a mere shadow of true existence. We are appendages, or "children", of the 4th dimensional spirit realm. Just like 2nd dimensional shadows are a result of 3rd beings, 3rd dimensional beings are a result of the 4th dimensional Being. Just like shadows temporarily fade from existence when there is no light, we too as 3rd dimensional beings temporarily fade from existence when we lose touch with the 4th dimensional Divine Image, God. When Adam and Eve deviated from the Image, they became subject to time, and would "...not be allowed to...take...from the tree of life and eat, and live forever" (Genesis 3:22), instead they would "...certainly die" (Genesis 2:17). Therefore, following the philosophy of Christ reintegrates us into the Divine Image with eternal life. This Image is the light.

Jesus said, "If they say to you, 'Where did you come from?', say to them, 'We came from the light, the place where the light came into being on its own accord and established itself and became manifest through their image.' If they say to you, 'Is it you?', say, 'We are its children, we are the elect of the living father.'

(Thomas 50)

It is no coincidence that many near death experiences cause visions of approaching a light. Einstein's analysis on the speed of light was groundbreaking, truly revolutionary. Through experiment, it was demonstrated that as an object approaches the speed of light, it begins to contract materially. Theoretically, when an object reaches the speed of light it would literally disappear. This is because the speed of light *is* the reference frame for all matter, and if you were to become the light you would become time fabric itself. Our brains must become tuned to this Divinity. Our 3rd dimensional being is an incident of the

4th dimension, and we have become entranced with the 3rd, forgetting we are part of the 4th. This is what Plato is trying to explain in his allegory of the cave. In Plato's cave allegory, the prisoners are entranced by the 2nd dimensional shadows. Through the pursuit of knowledge and Goodness they are able to break free and understand their true existence.

$E = mc^2$ is actually very simple. Experimentally, it was demonstrated that in every gram of matter, there is the speed of light squared amount of energy, or 90,000,000,000,000 Joules of energy per 1 g of matter. The energy consumption of the world in 2008 was 474,000,000,000,000,000,000 Joules of energy. This means that 5.3 million grams, or about 12,000 pounds of matter holds enough energy to satisfy the world's annual energy demand. This means that theoretically there is enough energy in one elephant to supply the entire world with energy for a year. The only problem is we do not know how to efficiently harness this energy.

$E = mc^2$ demonstrated that everything is energy. Mass is energy. More specifically, mass is very dense energy. All that *is*, is the same energy. Everything is one. Energy, vibration, sound or "the Word of God", is the basis of everything. The first thing God did from nothingness was create light. "And God said, 'Let there be light,' and there was light" (Genesis 1:3). Similarly, our scientific knowledge shows us that the big bang was an inexplicable expansion of light from a single point. How else would the writers of the bible know this? It must be Divine inspiration.

The speed of light, and light itself, is time, the 4th dimension, The Tree of Life, God. Our pineal gland has PHOTORECEPTORS! IT IS CAPABLE OF DETECTING LIGHT DESPITE IT BEING INSIDE THE SKULL ISOLATED FROM EXTERNAL LIGHT.

This is the neuroanatomical substrate for tapping into the kingdom of heaven, and essentially adjusting our consciousness to pure light. This is the internal light of God that we can activate through love, faith, and dissolving our egoic barrier through humility.

"This is the message we have heard from him and declare to you: God is light; in him there is no darkness at all. If we claim to have fellowship with him and yet walk in the darkness, we lie and do not live out the truth. But if we walk in the light, as he is in the light, we have fellowship with one another, and the blood of Jesus, his Son, purifies us from all sin."

(1 John 1:5-7)

The savior said, "O blessed Thomas, of course this visible light shines on your behalf - not in order that you remain here, but rather that you might come forth - and whenever all the elect abandon materiality, then this light will withdraw up to its essence, and its essence will welcome it, since it is a good servant."

(The book of Thomas the Contender by John D. Turner)

"The city (heaven) does not need the sun or the moon to shine on it, for the glory of God gives it light, and the Lamb is its lamp."

(Revelation 21:23)

"There will be no more night. They will not need

the light of a lamp or the light of the sun, for the Lord God will give them light. And they will reign for ever and ever."

(Revelation 22:5)

This also makes more sense of this aforementioned passage:

"...There is light within a person of light, and it shines on the whole world. If it does not shine, it is dark."

(Thomas 24).

We as imperfect humans are currently living in the physical 3rd dimension, with the potential to enter the spiritual 4th dimension. We are all on the verge of the 4th dimension, but our wicked ways have made us blind to this reality. We are on the spiritual frontier and are too distracted by materialism to explore it. We are given the opportunity to rise into the realm of spirit, but we are all missing the mark (sinning).

"Behold, all souls are Mine; the soul of the father as well as the soul of the son is Mine. The soul who sins will die."

(Ezekiel 18:4)

Do not think that your misdoings are unforgiveable. All can be forgiven through repentance, humility and understanding your wrongdoing. Pursue your individuality. Do not simply "be nice", rather, "be you". There is power in the truth, let your true self shine. Once you are certain that your ways are virtuous, you can join the flow of the universe without inhibition. When your ways are Just, there is no need to hesitate, because there is no need for a filter. Once you have purified your thoughts, you will be amazed at how perfectly everything flows. Forgive and love unconditionally. Do not be misled by the status quo. Especially the status quo of the scientific community. Many scientists have microscoped their world views and have become deluded from the larger picture, the grander truth.

Darwin's theory of evolution is a plausible explanation of how things came to be from a 3rd dimensional perspective, a perspective that is bound by time. The creation story presented in the bible is a 4th dimensional account of how things came to be, of which the only thing that we can accurately check with 3rd dimensional science is the first visible step. The first visible action was God creating light out of formlessness, which is referred to as the big bang. God, as a 4th dimensional entity, the embodiment of light, and the totality of the spiritual realm is unrestrained by time:

"A thousand years in the sight of the Lord is like a day that has just gone by…"

(Psalm 90:4)

"But do not forget this one thing, dear friends: with the Lord a day is like a thousand years, and a thousand years are like a day."

(2 Peter 3:8)

Before the fall of Adam and Eve, they were eternal beings. They were created as 4th dimensional beings in God's Image in the Light, but their participation in imperfection, or evil, caused them to lose touch with the divine and delve into darkness. The tree of life is a reference to this 4th dimension, or spiritual realm, whereas the tree of the knowledge of good and evil is a reference to the 3rd dimension, the dimension of decay, in which people die. We were meant to be pioneers of the spiritual realm, but we are all distracted by physical matters such as money:

"Treasure not up to yourselves treasures on the earth, where moth and rust disfigure, and where thieves break through and steal,

but treasure up to yourselves treasures in heaven, where neither moth nor rust doth disfigure, and where thieves do not break through nor steal,

for where your treasure is, there will be also your heart.

`The lamp of the body is the eye, if, therefore, thine eye may be perfect, all thy body shall be enlightened,

but if thine eye may be evil, all thy body shall be dark; if, therefore, the light that [is] in thee is darkness -- the darkness, how great!

`None is able to serve two lords, for either he will hate the one and love the other, or he will hold to the one, and despise the other; ye are not able to serve God and Mammon (money)."

(Matthew 6:19-24 YLT)

Notice how 'eye' is singular in this verse? In Young's Literal Translation, eye is singular throughout this passage. This is not referring to our two eyes. Rather, this is a reference to the pineal gland, which is referred to as the 3rd eye. Where our body becomes enlightened. Remember how the pineal gland literally has photoreceptors? This is the inner frontier to the realm of light and Spirit.

Entering the spiritual realm may require help from the opposite gender. The etymology of Elohim, the creator God in Genesis, is quite interesting. Elohim is a Hebrew word, the root 'El' is Hebrew for 'God' which is in the masculine form. The feminine form of 'El' is 'Eloah', meaning 'Goddess'. Elohim is plural; therefore it literally means Gods and Godesses, Male and Female. To further demonstrate the plurality of Elohim:

Then Elohim said, "Let us make humans in **our** image, in **our** likeness..."

(Genesis 1:26 NOG)

This androgenous, plural entity was spliced into male and female. This makes sense, especially when we consider how every particle in nature has a corresponding anti-particle. Einstein claims:

"...the following requirement for a complete theory seems to be a necessary one: *every element of the physical reality must have a counterpart in the physical theory.*" [8]

Humans, i.e. fallen Gods, are no exception to this rule. When you consider how to make something out of nothing, this makes sense. When there is nothing, or "0", split it into "-1" and "+1".

$$0 = -1 + 1$$

Both matter and the human prototype were made in this way. This created the world of duality in which we currently reside. Our journey through life is a gradual homecoming, exemplified by Homer's Odyssey, in which we reunite with our eternal counterpart. So, why is there such enmity and hostility between male and female? Examining sub-atomic particles can give us some insight.

Think of the proton and the electron. One is positive and the other negative. So, why do they not unite? Why does the negatively charged electron orbit around its beloved positively charged nucleus? A similar question can be asked regarding the human male and female. What separates us? It is the ego, or sin, that generates such separation. This disallows a true union of male and female. Male and female is like a lock and key model to the secrets of the universe. A true union of male and female, based in love and selflessness, helps us enter the spiritual realm of light and love.

"...at the beginning the Creator made them male and female, and said, 'For this reason a man will... be united to his wife, and the two will become on flesh' So they are no longer two, but one flesh. Therefore what God has joined together, let no one separate"

(Matthew 19:4-6)

Wherefore, remember, that ye [were] once the nations in the flesh... that ye were at that time apart from Christ, having been alienated from the commonwealth of Israel (spiritual realm), and strangers to the covenants of the promise, having no hope, and without God, in the world; and now, in Christ Jesus, ye being once afar off became nigh in the blood of the Christ, for he is our peace, who did **make both one**, and the middle wall of the enclosure (ego) did break down, the enmity in his flesh, the law of the commands in ordinances having done away, **that the two he might create in himself into one new man**, making peace, and might reconcile both in **one body** to

God through the cross, having slain the enmity in it, and having come, he did proclaim good news -- peace to you -- the far-off and the nigh, because through him we have the access -- **we both** -- in one Spirit unto the Father. Then, therefore, ye are no more strangers and foreigners, but fellow-citizens of the saints, and of the household of God, being built upon the foundation of the apostles and prophets, Jesus Christ himself being chief corner-[stone], in whom all the building fitly framed together doth increase to a holy sanctuary in the Lord, in whom also ye are builded together, for a habitation of God in the Spirit."

(Ephesians 2:11-22 YLT)

As long as we remain diligent on the path, we receive such a gift. The gift is to unionize with the opposite gender and venture off into the spiritual realm in love as one. What better gift? You get to share an eternity with the love of your life. Plato explains the coming of such love, and he calls it the ladder of love. Plato notes that the pursuance of philosophy, an understanding of the Divine, allows us to understand our true self. Once you understand yourself, you naturally attract a likewise mate. As you progress on the path, and understand your true self through purifying your thoughts, you emanate the signal of your soul for your eternal mate to receive. It is like human magnetism. Remember, you reap what you sow; you attract, or repel, your eternal soul mate depending on how true you are to yourself. A true union of male and female creates a spiritual offspring. Think of it like a sperm forming with the egg. Prior to fertilization they are simply male and female cells, but once they unite they give birth to an entity much higher in complexity; a human. Similarly, a male and female human must unite, in love without their egos, and give birth to an entity much higher in complexity; a spiritual creation. The spiritual offspring of humankind; The Son of Man. A sexual perversion disallows this union. This is why adultery is so detrimental to our being. It disallows the natural reunion of the soul:

"My son, pay attention to my wisdom,
  turn your ear to my words of insight,
that you may maintain discretion
  and your lips may preserve knowledge.
For the lips of the adulterous woman drip honey,
  and her speech is smoother than oil;
but in the end she is bitter as gall,
  sharp as a double-edged sword.
Her feet go down to death;
  her steps lead straight to the grave.
She gives no thought to the way of life;
  her paths wander aimlessly, but she does not know it…

  For lack of discipline they will die,
led astray by their own great folly." (Psalm 5)

Adultery blocks the way of life and leads to death. The story of the Samaritan woman in John 4 exemplifies this. The woman had multiple husbands, of which none were her true mate. The Samaritan woman was fetching water out of a well when Jesus told her:

"Everyone who drinks this water will be thirsty again, but whoever drinks the water I give them will never thirst. Indeed, the water I give them will become in them a spring of water welling up to eternal life."

The woman responded, "Sir, give me this water so that I won't get thirsty and have to keep coming here to draw water."

Jesus told her, "Go, call your husband and come back."

"I have no husband," she replied

Jesus said to her, "You are right when you say you have no husband. The fact is, you have had five husbands, and the man you now have is not your husband..."

When the woman asked where to get the water of eternal life, Jesus told her to get her spouse. But, she never had a true husband, her soul mate, instead they were relationships of lust. Just like Adam and Eve were created from splitting the Androgynous Soul of Elohim, we as humans reunite with this Image with our soul mate into the realm of spirit. Now is a good time to reiterate: "...a man leaves his father and mother and is united to his wife, and they become **one flesh**" (Genesis 2:24). Some may say this is referring to physical sex, but the context of the passage makes this very unlikely. This passage is shortly after the human soul is split into male and female. This is referring to the idea that a return to Eden will occur when Male and Female truly reunite. This theme arises in Platonic philosophy when Aristophanes discusses the idea of a soul mate.

"The original human nature was not like the present, but different. The sexes were not two as they are now, but originally three in number; there was man, woman, and the union of the two, of which the name survives but nothing else. Once it was a distinct kind, with a bodily shape and a name of its own, constituted by the union of the male and the female: but now only the word 'androgynous' is preserved, and that as a term of reproach... due to a struggle of power, (God) spoke and cut the male-female union in two... After the division of male and female, each began desiring the other half, and came together, entwined in mutual embraces, longing to grow into one... So ancient is the desire of one another which is implanted in us, reuniting our original nature, seeking to make one of two, and to heal the state of mankind... And the reason is that human nature was originally one and we were a whole, and the desire and pursuit of the whole is called love. There was a time, I say, when we were one, but now because of the wickedness of mankind God has dispersed us... And if we are not obedient to the heavenly matters, there is a danger that we shall be split up again... Wherefore let us exhort to piety in all things, that we may avoid evil and obtain the good, taking Love for our leader and commander... Wherefore, if we would praise him who has given to us the benefit, we must praise the god Love, who is our greatest benefactor, both leading us in this life back to our own nature, and giving us high hopes for the future, for he promises that if we are pious, he will restore us to our original state, and heal us and make us happy and blessed."

(Plato's Symposium 189c-193e)

The true purpose of the male and female union may not be to beget physical children, but rather a spiritual offspring. Physical child birth did not occur until the fall of Adam and Eve:

God said to Eve,

"I will make your pains in childbearing very severe;
    with painful labor you will give birth to children."

(Genesis 3:16)

Childbearing only occurred after Adam and Eve became lost in the physical world. It is through a spiritual offspring that we can return to where we once were. The mystery of male and female uniting to form a spiritual offspring is discussed thoroughly in the Gospel of Philip:

"All those who practice the sacred embrace will kindle the light; they will not beget as people do in ordinary marriages, which take place in darkness." (Line 126)

"[We] are reborn by the Christ two by two. In his Breath, we experience a new embrace; we are no longer in duality, but in unity." (Line 74)

"All will be clothed in light when they enter into the mystery of the sacred embrace." (Line 77)

"What is the bridal chamber, if not the place of trust and consciousness in the embrace? It is an icon of Union, beyond all forms of possession; here is where the veil is torn from top to bottom; **here is where some arise and awaken**." (Line 76)

"When Eve was in Adam, there was no death; when she was separated from him, death came. If she enters back into him, and he accepts her, there will be no more death..." (Line 71)

"[Jesus came] to the place of separation so as to reunite all that had been separated in God." (Line 72)

"Seek the experience of undefiled intercourse; it has great power." (Line 60)

"From heaven the Father sent her her man, who is her brother (soul mate), the firstborn. Then the bridegroom came down to the bride....Since that marriage is not like the carnal marriage... *And as if it were a burden they leave behind them the annoyance of physical desire....*[Once] they unite [with one another], they become a single life....For they were originally joined to one another when they were with the Father before the woman led astray the man, who is her brother (soul mate). This marriage has brought them back together again and the soul has been joined to her true love...." [9].

"[Through] the sacred embrace, we are invited into the interior. As long as this is hidden, unhappiness prevails; it always poisons the seeds [sperma], and evil is at work." (Line 125)

"If someone experiences Trust and Consciousness in the heart of the embrace, they become a child of light. If someone does not receive these, it is because they remain attached to what they know; when they cease to be attached, they will be able to receive them." (Line 127)

And finally...

"If woman had not been separated from man, she would not die with man. Her separation was at the origin of death. Christ comes again to heal this wound, to rediscover the lost unity, to enliven those who kill themselves in separation, reviving them in union." (Line 78)

This is what is meant by being born again. The spiritual birth, uniting with the kingdom of Heaven:

Jesus replied, "Very truly I tell you, no one can see the kingdom of God unless they are born again."

"How can someone be born when they are old?" Nicodemus asked. "Surely they cannot enter a second time into their mother's womb to be born!"

Jesus answered, "Very truly I tell you, no one can enter the kingdom of God unless they are born of water and the Spirit. **Flesh gives birth to flesh, but the Spirit gives birth to spirit**"

    (John 3:4-6)

    This is the Son of Man, the spiritual child that can be birthed by the human Mind:

"Now that you have purified yourselves by obeying the truth so that you have sincere love for each other, love one another deeply, from the heart. For you have been born again, not of perishable seed, but of imperishable through the living and enduring word of God"

    (1 Peter 1:22-23).

"Then when she becomes young again, she will ascend, praising the father and her brother (soul mate), by whom she was rescued. Thus it is by being born again that the soul will be saved"

    (exegesis of the soul by William C Robinson)

It is no coincidence that Mary Magdalene was the first person that Jesus came to after his resurrection (Mark 16:9). Mary Magdalene was very special to Jesus, and the misogynist leaders of the church at the time were hell-bent on hiding this concept. This is partially why the Gnostic Gospels have been dispelled from orthodox dogma. In the gospel of Mary Magdalene, the apostles argue about Mary Magdalene:

"...if the Savior made her worthy, who are you indeed to reject her? Surely the Savior knows her very well. That is why He loved her more than us."

(Mary Magdalene 9:8-9)

A true union between male and female is vital to spiritual progress. When talking to the woman at the well, Jesus claimed that whoever drinks the water he gives, Spirit, will never thirst. Does he mean this literally?

Later in John 4, the disciples are concerned that Jesus has not eaten, so his disciples urged him, "Rabbi, eat something" (John 4:31). Jesus responds, "I have food to eat that you know nothing about" (John 4:32). Fasting is believed to free us from carnality, and open up our souls to the power of innate spiritual nourishment. This is the food that Jesus is referring to, the Divine Source. The power of this spiritual, Divine sustenance is demonstrated by Jesus in the desert. The devil, otherwise known as material temptation, tested Jesus after he had fasted for forty days and forty nights in the wilderness:

The tempter came to him and said, "If you are the Son of God, tell these stones to become bread."

Jesus answered, "It is written: 'Man shall not live on bread alone, but on every word that comes from the mouth of God'"

(Matthew 4:3-4).

Living by the word of God presents infinite power, and this is why Jesus is tempted with the power and splendor of this world. It is his fasted state which empowers spirit. Jesus was tempted with all worldly pleasures because his pure unencumbered spirit allowed him immense power:

The devil took him to a very high mountain and showed him all the kingdoms of the world and their splendor. "All this I will give you," he said, "if you will bow down and worship me"

(Matthew 3:9).

Jesus chooses temperance:

Jesus said to him, "Away from me, Satan! For it is written: 'Worship the Lord your God, and serve him only.'"

Then the devil left him, and angels came and attended him.

(Matthew 3:10-11).

This demonstrates the power that coincides with dematerializing yourself through fasting, among other means. This makes sense of the last supper. This is literally Jesus' last meal before he begins fasting, gets crucified and rises from the dead:

When the hour came, Jesus and his apostles reclined at the table. And he said to them, "I have eagerly desired to eat this

Passover with you before I suffer. **For I tell you, I will not eat it again until it finds fulfillment in the kingdom of God."**

(Luke 22:14-16).

These themes also occur in Greek Philosophy. Diotima, a prophetess, explains to Socrates a dematerializing ascent in which the Divine becomes revealed:

"Whoever has been initiated so far in the mysteries of Love and has viewed all these aspects of the beautiful in due succession, is at last drawing near the **final revelation**. And now... there bursts upon him that wondrous vision which is the very soul of the beauty he has toiled so long for. It is an **everlasting** loveliness which neither comes nor goes, which neither flowers nor fades, for such beauty is the same on every hand, the same then as now, here as there, this way as that way, the same to every worshiper as it is to every other.

Nor will his vision of the beautiful take the form of a face, or of hands, or of anything that is of the flesh. It will be neither words, nor knowledge, nor a something that exists in something else, such as a living creature, or the earth, or the heavens, or anything that is--but subsisting of itself and by itself in an **eternal oneness**, while every lovely thing partakes of it in such sort that, however much the parts may wax and wane, it will be neither more nor less, but still the same inviolable whole.

And so, when his prescribed devotion to boyish beauties has carried our candidate so far that the universal beauty dawns upon his **inward sight**, he is almost within reach of the final revelation. And this is the way, the only way, he must approach, or be led toward, the sanctuary of **Love**. Starting from individual beauties, the quest for the universal beauty must find him ever mounting the **heavenly ladder**, stepping from rung to rung--that is, from one to two, and from two to every lovely body, from bodily beauty to the beauty of institutions, from institutions to learning, and from learning in general to the special lore that pertains to nothing but the beautiful itself--until at last he comes to know what beauty is.

And if, my dear Socrates, Diotima went on, man's life is ever worth the living, it is when he has attained this vision of the very soul of beauty. And once you have seen it, you will never be seduced again by the charm of gold, of dress, of comely boys, or lads just ripening to manhood; you will care nothing for the beauties that used to take your breath away and kindle such a longing in you, and many others like you, Socrates, to be always at the side of the beloved and feasting your eyes upon him, so that you would be content, if it were possible, to **deny yourself the grosser necessities of meat and drink**, so long as you were with him.

But if it were given to man to gaze on beauty's very self--unsullied, unalloyed, and freed from the mortal taint that haunts the frailer loveliness of flesh and blood--if, I say, it were given to man to see the heavenly beauty face to face, would you call his, she asked me, an unenviable life, whose eyes had been opened to the vision, and who had gazed upon it in true contemplation until it had become his own forever?

And remember, she said, that it is when he looks upon beauty's visible presentment, and only then, that a man will be quickened with the true, and not the seeming, virtue--for it is virtue's self that quickens him, not virtue's semblance. And when he has brought forth and reared this perfect virtue, he shall be called the friend of god, and **if ever it is given to man to put on immortality, it shall be given to him.**"

(Plato's Symposium 211-212)

So, is fasting a part of the ascent out of the world of materialism? This seems to make sense from a scientific perspective as well. Calorie restricted rats, that is, rats that were not allowed to eat as much as they wanted, had an increased lifespan of about 50%. In other words, rats that fasted lived 50% longer than rats that were allowed to eat freely. During food digestion, there is an increased blood supply to the gut to help digest food. When there is no food to be digested, this blood supply can be allocated elsewhere. This allows higher cognitive processing due to an increase blood volume allowed in the brain. Although, this may have an opposite effect if you are enthralled by food. I used to be unable to leave the house if I did not eat breakfast. I had enslaved myself to food, and if I missed breakfast I felt like I was starving to death by 10 a.m. This is all a mentality, a mindset that you must overcome. Once I realized this was unnecessary, I no longer felt the ravenous hunger.

Eating heavy foods anchors you to the material realm. Abstaining from food hastens your ascent. The Buddha fasted for 49 days before reaching enlightenment. All genuine, spiritually inspired establishments praise fasting due to its empowering effects. Jesus mentions multiple times that this is a supplement for spiritual growth. The fact that a fasted state was present when Jesus was offered endless material power in the desert, and also during Jesus' death and resurrection implies that fasting is immensely powerful. This is how Jesus "fed" thousands with 5 loaves and two fish, it was not with literal food, but with food of the Spirit. This event occurred during the Passover, which is a peculiar celebration that deserves some elaboration.

A Passover seems to be eluding to a spiritual awakening, a passing over into a new state of consciousness. There are clues in the bible as to when this sort of mass spiritual awakening is scheduled to happen, and apparently it has happened before. "Let there be lights in the vault of the sky to separate the day from the night, **and let them serve as signs to mark sacred times, and days and years...**" (Genesis 1:14). Creation yielded a built-in clock that can be used to determine when sacred events are to occur. The timing of these sacred events are revealed throughout the bible. In the bible, these times are indicated by mentioning various signs of the zodiac.

These signs of the zodiac correspond to various ages that span a couple thousand years. The zodiac constellations are referred to because they cannot be misconstrued like a man-made calendar. The first mentioning occurs in the book of Exodus. When Moses and his people are awaiting to enter the Promised Land, they are told "Only when the ram's horn sounds a long blast may they approach the mountain" (Exodus 19:13); this would be the time when the lord would descend upon the mountain. The ram's horn is symbolic of the constellation Aries, which is a ram and its symbol is literally ram's horns. This would astrologically put the time of Moses at about 2200 B.C. A couple thousand years later, around 0 A.D., Jesus was roaming the earth. This was around the start of the age of Pisces, which is represented by two fish. Ring any bells? "Taking the five loaves and the **two fish** and looking up to heaven, he gave thanks and broke the loaves. Then he gave them to his disciples to distribute to the people. He also divided the two fish among them all." As stated before, here Jesus is not referring to actual food. The two fish is referring to the new age of Pisces, which astrologically dawns around 0 A.D. In light of all that has been said so far, John 6 is worth examining in more detail:

"**The Passover was near**... When Jesus looked up and saw a great crowd coming toward him, he said to Philip, "Where shall we buy bread for these people to eat?" He asked this only to test him, for he already had in mind what he was going to do. Philip answered him, "It would take more than a half a year's wages to buy enough bread for each one to have a bite!" Another of his disciples, Andrew, spoke up, "Here is a boy with five small barley loaves and two small fish, but how far will they go among so many?"

(John 6:4-9)

Jesus is not about to multiply food, but rather feed people with the unperishable food of Spirit. The people were so amazed by the power of Spirit that they sought out Jesus:

"When they found him on the other side of the lake, they asked him, "Rabbi, when did you get here?" Jesus answered, Very truly I tell you, you are looking for me, not because you saw the sign I performed but because you ate the loaves and had your fill. Do not work for food that spoils, but for food that endures to eternal life, which the **Son of Man** will give you. For on him God the Father has placed his seal of approval."

(John 6:25-27)

The people are skeptical, so Jesus reiterates:

"No one came come to me unless the Father who sent me draws them, and I will raise them up... Everyone who has heard the Father and learned from him comes to me... Very truly I tell you, the one who believes has eternal life. I am the bread of life. Your ancestors ate the manna in the wilderness, yet they died. But here is the bread that comes down from heaven, which anyone may eat and not die. I am the living bread that came down from heaven. Whoever eats this bread will live forever."

(John 6:44-51)

The bread that came from heaven is spiritual sustenance. Bread is used as a metaphor. Bread is the risen product of dough. Jesus is the bread of life; that which can be risen from humanity. This is why Jesus broke bread and gave it to his disciples; this is a metaphysical transformation that he gave to his disciples. Anyone can raise the bread of life and do as Jesus did. So, can we actually live without material food? Let's take a look.

Melanin is a pigment present in our skin cells. It is "...capable of dissipating >99.9% of absorbed UV and visible radiation..." and allocating this energy into a useful form [10]. This energy is used to split water into diatomic Hydrogen and Oxygen [11].

$$H_2O_{(l)} \rightleftharpoons H_{2(g)} + 1/2\ O_{2(g)}$$

$$\Delta H: 286\ kJ/mol$$

This means that for every mol of water that is split, 286 kJ of energy is absorbed into the system. The human body requires on average about 8700 kJ of energy per day.

$$8700\ kJ / (286\ kJ/mol) = 30.4\ mol\ of\ water$$

Theoretically, this means that 30.4 mols of water, or 548 mL of water, **with adequate sunlight** could satisfy the daily energy needs of the average human. The energy formed from this reaction resides in H_2. Diatomic hydrogen (H_2) is the energy of the future not just for the human body, but also for electrical generation. There are a plethora of books that discuss the energy potential of diatomic hydrogen. Just like humanity must begin to refrain from the unsustainable combustion engine, the human itself must escape the confines of its own combustion engine that runs on food, and seek a new source of energy;

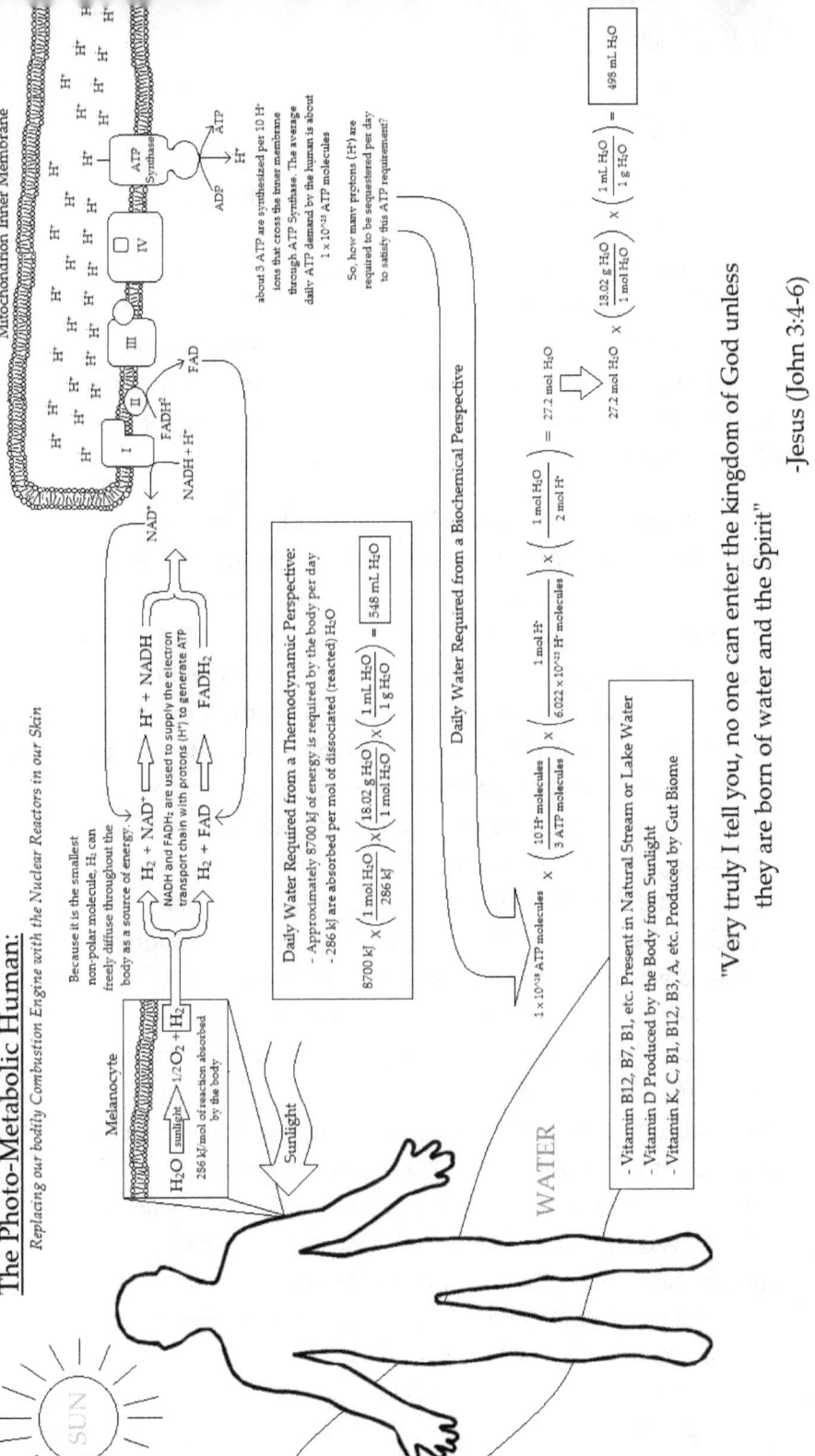

water and sunlight.

Diatomic hydrogen, being the smallest non-polar molecule, has the highest cell membrane permeability. This implies that the H_2 formed from this reaction can easily spread throughout the entire body as available energy. H_2 is direct fuel for the electron transport chain of the human mitochondrion via the reduction of FAD or NAD^+ and results in the production of ATP. ATP is the body's universal energy currency. To top it all off, H_2 is the best antioxidant known to man [12].

Skeptics may wonder where we would get nutrients without food. The Kreb's cycle describes the molecular changes that occur to form energy from glucose (food). This process is mostly reversible, and therefore there is a potential for humans to synthesize glucose and other macronutrients via reduction of CO_2 by H_2. The abundance of $NADH^+$ and $FADH_2$ from the H_2 formed by the splicing of water would supply adequate energy for the synthesis of these macromolecules. Carbohydrates and fatty acids can be produced by atmospheric CO_2, $NADH^+$, and ATP through the reversal of the Kreb's cycle. Atmospheric nitrogen, the most abundant gas in our earthly air, commonly thought to be useless to humans, could react with H_2 to form ammonia which is a precursor to amino acid synthesis. Ammonia can react with various carbohydrates to synthesize amino acids (protein). It seems likely that our metabolism can make a transcendent shift to relying solely on water, sunlight and atmospheric gases for sustenance. I have not been able to test this yet because it is currently winter as I write this. Although, there have been plenty of people who have claimed to have lived without food for years such as Ram Bahadur Bomjon, Jasmuheen, The Buddha, and the Rosicrucians. I am not certain that this is a necessity, but I am certain that a water fast can expedite spiritual progress.

Furthermore, natural water from a natural stream or lake, the original water source for humanity, is packed with nutrients such as vitamin B12, biotin, thiamine, etc [13]. Our skin also produces Vitamin D naturally with sunlight, Vitamin D also regulates the gut biome [14]. A regulated gut biome is important because these bacteria that live in our gut that provide us with vital nutrients such as Vitamin K [15], Vitamin B1, Vitamin B12, Vitamin B3, Vitamin B7 [16], Vitamin A [17], etc. Human metabolism in a fasted state may be much more efficient. Fasting is seldom studied by science, so metabolic changes may be occurring during a fasted state that increases nutrient retention and recycling. So, does Jesus mean we literally don't need food? From a scientific standpoint, it seems like it may be possible, but more research is required. **If you are going to try this be careful, it may only be possible for the spiritually adept and those who truly believe it is possible.** Be sure to drink unpolluted stream water and get adequate sun. The farther upstream the water source is, the less likely it is polluted. Be wary of synthetic run-off from nearby farms.

Those of you familiar with the bible may be saying, wait a minute, Adam and Eve were able to eat from the tree of life in paradise. Yes, but this is likely a symbolic form of eating, just like the symbolic eating when Jesus "fed" the thousands with 5 loaves of bread. Here they are consuming Godly sustenance, pure good energy:

Jesus asked, "You of little faith, why are you talking among yourselves about having no bread? Do you still not understand? Don't you remember the five loaves for the five thousand, and how many basketfuls you gathered? Or the seven loaves for the four thousand, and how many basketfuls you gathered? How is it you don't understand that I was not talking to you about bread?

(Matthew 16:8-11)

It was by eating, or general participation in materiality, the tree of knowledge of good and evil that we lost touch with the spiritual realm. It is an enthrallment with the material world that caused us to lose touch with the spiritual world. When Adam and Eve partook in materiality they forgot their spiritual origins and would surely die:

"The serpent hath caused me to forget – and I do eat."

(Genesis 3:13 YLT)

An indulgence in materiality caused us to forget our spiritual origins. Remember Socrates' Theory of Recollection? We are meant to remember our spiritual origin. But we as a species forgot this long ago. Think about it. If forgetting means to not know, then knowledge is simply a remembrance. This knowledge is within us. An escape from materiality allows us to remember, or know, the spiritual realm. Déjà vu is us remembering our timeless spiritual existence. Remember the section above mentioning gamma waves and how they are correlated to an elevated consciousness? The occurrence of Déjà vu is strongly correlated with gamma waves [18]. Déjà vu is also experienced consistently by those who take magic mushrooms. When we experience déjà vu we are beginning to enter the spirit realm, but unfortunately this experience is often fleeting. From my own experience, material thoughts (sexual perversion, food, etc.) or disregarding the present causes the déjà vu to end. Déjà vu needs to be ridden like a wave; go with the flow. Here are some interesting biblical passages regarding déjà vu:

"What has been is what will be, and what has been done is what will be done, and there is nothing new under the sun. Is there a thing of which it is said, "See, this is new"? It has been already in the ages before us."

(Ecclesiastes 1:9-10 ESV)

"The whole He hath made beautiful in its season; also, that knowledge He hath put in their heart without which man findeth not out the work that God hath done from the beginning even unto the end."

(Ecclesiastes 3:11 YLT)

"For no prophecy was ever produced by the will of man, but men spoke from God as they were carried along by the Holy Spirit."

(2 Peter 1:21 ESV)

Déjà vu is the remembrance and the coming of the Son of Man. The Son of Man, the spiritual offspring, requires no food. A water fast releases your material anchor, and helps to reveal the spiritual Son of Man within.

"Very truly I tell you, no one can enter the kingdom of God unless they are born of **water** and the Spirit."

(John 3:4-6).

There is another mass spiritual awakening coming soon, just like the one in John 6 with the two fish during the dawn of Pisces. In The Gospel of Mark, Jesus makes an astrological reference for when the next awakening would occur. When Jesus' disciples ask him where the next Passover will occur, Jesus says:

"Go into the city and **a man carrying a jar of water** will meet you. Follow Him"

(Mark 14:13).

Here Jesus is referring to the Aquarius constellation. Aquarius is the water bearer, which is depicted by a man with a jar of water, which is the age that humanity is currently entering. Aries, Pisces, and Aquarius are all mentioned in reference to a Passover. In the precession of the equinox, which the bible uses to date events, it goes chronologically Aries, Pisces, and then Aquarius. In the beginning of the Age of Aries it was Moses' people entering the Promised Land symbolized by the ram's horn. During the era of Pisces, approximately 0 AD, it was Jesus showing the people a world beyond materialism symbolized by feeding them with two fish (Pisces). Now, when the disciples asked Jesus where the **next** Passover would occur, he told them it would be with the water bearer, the Age of Aquarius, the age we are currently entering. The Passover, which is mentioned for each of these references to the zodiac, is the Passing over into the kingdom of heaven. A mass spiritual awakening.

In the Metaphysical Bible Dictionary, The Passover is described:

"The Passover was used by Jesus to represent the freeing of the spiritual man from the dominion of sense. It is part of the regenerative process that goes on in the body under the inspiration of the Christ mind. It is the passing over or out of one state of consciousness into another" (p. 503).

This is why Jesus is considered the Passover lamb for humanity. He was the sacrifice for all the wickedness of the world so that humanity could pass over into the spiritual existence. The Mayans had this spiritual transcendence understood very well. They constructed a calendar which resembled Divine cycles. They predicted the dawn of the next age to be around December 2012, remember the mass hysteria behind this? Many viewed this as a doomsday, but it was actually a beginning to a new cycle. December 2012, which is around the dawn of Aquarius, marked the beginning of a gradual process in which humankind would begin to awaken to its Divine Origin. The fact that the Mayans and Jesus were able to predict a spiritual awakening to occur at the same time, despite being geographically isolated by AN OCEAN, is fascinating. Yet again, I see no other explanation except Divine Inspiration. So, what will it be like when we awaken to the world of spirit?

      Every night we experience a taste of the spiritual realm. It is the realm that transcends time because it is time; the 4th dimension. Every night we dream, and in our dreams time is irrelevant. This is a taste of what is to come. Although I am only speculating, I would bet integration into heaven would be much like a dream with the control we possess while awake, a merging of our wake and dream state to be explored with our eternal mate. Neuroscience has realized that the same conscious stream that is active during your wake state, is also what is active during your dream state. According to your brain, there is no difference in perception between your awake and dream state. Despite being the same perception, there are other modulatory and inhibitory circuits which are active during your wake state. We are limiting our own potential due to our own inhibitions, or faithlessness. In such a realm we would have the power to, for example, move a mountain, or whatever you wish, "...Nothing will be impossible for you" (Matthew 17:20). But, only if we truly believe we could, just like how a dream works. "Everything is possible for one who believes" (Mark 9:23). Attaining such a state involves us waking up from our selfish wicked ways, and believing we are part of something larger, and believing we have the ability.

Let me try to summarize with a scientific analogy. Atoms aggregate together to create molecules, a more complex entity is created by this union. These molecules then aggregate in a structured manner to create cells. Cells aggregate in a structured manner to create complex multicellular organisms, humans. The next step is for the race of human beings to incorporate through love and emerge as a singular unionized entity in the light. The power of light and love is beginning to overpower the evil in the world:

"The old appeals to racial, sexual, and religious chauvinism, to rabid nationalist fervor are beginning not to work. A new consciousness is developing that sees the earth as a **single organism** and recognizes that an organism at war with itself is doomed."

-Carl Sagan

To give an example of this earth-human synchrony I have to briefly discuss the periodic table of elements. In the periodic table, atoms in the same column share similar characteristics. For example, bronze, silver, and gold share the same column of the periodic table. Carbon, which is the basis of all life on earth, is in the same column and directly above silicon in the periodic table. Silicon is the key component to computers, and thus artificial intelligence. Silicon can be thought of as the earth's conscious substrate. It's as if the earth is using humanity to build its intelligent capabilities. This is why crystals have been popular with the new age moment. Even more peculiar are the quartz crystal (silicon) skulls which have generated a lot of anecdotal theories regarding their origin and purpose. There is a synchronization in which humans have used silicon to make computers which have rapidly advanced our conscious evolution. This ultimately gave rise to the internet; the most useful tool for our understanding. I would not have been able to write this, and you would not be reading this if not for the internet. We are no longer geographically limited in our understanding. The internet has acted as an artificial tether for humanity. Through silicon-based computers, the earth gave humanity a boost in reaching a more adaptive understanding.

To think the earth is not alive would be naïve. Think of all life. It has one thing in common, water. All living things are about 2/3 water. Similarly, the earth is about 2/3 water. Rivers, arteries, and roots; it is all alive. Our current state in humanity is making the earth sick. Eventually, there will be backlash from the planet if we continue our ravenous wastefulness. Do not worry about others so much, but rather focus on yourself. You are the one who is shaping the external environment. It is your internal conflict which causes external conflict. You are the external world. Atman is Brahman. If a tree falls in the woods does it make a sound? There is no conscious observer to record it. It was not the environment that evolved the observer, it was the observer that made the environment from consciousness:

"In the beginning of God's preparing the heavens and the earth – the earth hath existed waste and void, and darkness is on the face of the deep, and the Spirit of God fluttering (meaning pulsating, or vibrating) on the face of the waters, and God saith, 'Let light be;' and light is."

(Genesis 1:1-3 YLT)

Remember how Einstein's equation demonstrated that *everything* is varying densities of energy, or vibration? This vibration has always existed, and it is God, the Alpha and Omega. We are all a part of it, and we must regain harmony with this Divine Energy. The world exists as a probabilistic waveform until an observer makes an observation. This was demonstrated in the double-slit photon light experiment, and was described by theorists as quantum entanglement. This conundrum is demonstrated by Schrodinger's cat which poses a simple question; if a cat is inside a box, is it dead or alive? You cannot know until an observation is made by opening the box. Prior to observing whether or not the cat is alive, the cat's livelihood exists as a probabilistic wave. Therefore, the unobserved world exists as a waveform, and it is an observer that collapses this waveform into a sensible form. This is why belief is so powerful. With doubtless faith, one can craft their world. This is demonstrated when Jesus convinces a man that his son is healed:

The royal official said, "Sir, come down before my child dies."

"Go," Jesus replied, "your son will live."

The man took Jesus at his word and departed. While he was still on the way, his servants met him with the news that his boy was living. When he inquired as to the time when his son got better, they said to him, "Yesterday, at one in the afternoon, the fever left him."

Then the father realized that this was the exact time at which Jesus had said to him, "Your son will live." So he and his whole household believed.

(John 4:49-53)

The royal official, upon truly believing his son would be healed, physically manifested a world where his son was healed.

This healing occurred at the exact time that he believed his son would be healed. Amazing.

The first chapter of John is incredibly enlightening, especially regarding all that has been discussed so far:

"In the beginning was the Word (vibration), and the Word was with God, and the Word was God. He was with God in the beginning. Through him all things were made; without him nothing was made that has been made. In him was life, and that life was the light of all mankind. The light shines in the darkness, and the darkness has not overcome it.

There was a man sent from God whose name was John. He came as a witness to testify concerning that light, so that through him all might believe. He himself was not the light; he came only as a witness to the light.

The true light that gives light to everyone was coming into the world. He was in the world, and though the world was made through him, the world did not recognize him. He came to that which was his own, but his own did not receive him. Yet to all who did receive him, to those who believed in his name, he gave the right to become children of God— children born not of natural descent, nor of human decision or a husband's will, but **born of God.**"

(John 1:1-13)

Let's conclude. Once the external was created, the Image of Elohim incarnated Itself. These God Incarnates, Adam and Eve, were one with their environment. It was when they became enthralled with their environment, materiality, that they lost their spiritual connection. Humanity remained lost and subject to a world of decay until the coming of Christ, who told us that our world is an illusion, and that there is a higher truth to our existence. He demonstrated the unlimited human potential, and reminded us that we are all Sons of God and are capable of returning to paradise. Few believed, and many remained entranced by materiality. Since free will remains, so does sin. People only receive evil if they choose it. It is through sin that we lose Divine sustenance and become subject to death. It is through love, humility and faith that we can return home to Eternity. Which will you choose?

"Very truly I tell you, whoever hears my word and believes him who sent me has eternal life and will not be judged but has crossed over from death to life."

(John 5:24)

References:

1) Inventions of Nikola Tesla: A Complete Set of Patents. (2014) Page 443.
2) Luke et al. (2012). A sideways look at the neurobiology of Psi: precognition and circadian rhythms. Neuroquantology, 10 (3), 580-590.
3) Sahai et al. (2013). Pineal gland: A structural and functional enigma 2013. Journal of Anatomical Society of India, 62 (2), 170-177.
4) Sayin et al. A comparative review of the neuro-psychopharmacology of hallucinogen-induced altered states of consciousness: The uniqueness of some hallucinogens. The Interdisciplinary Journal of Neuroscience and Quantum Physics, 10 (2), (2012).
5) Muthukumaraswamy et al. (2013) Broadband cortical desynchronization underlies the human psychedelic state. Journal of Neuroscience, 33 (38), 15171-15183.
6) Vazquez MA, Jin J, Dauwels J, Vialette FB. (2013). Automated detection of paroxysmal gamma waves in meditation EEG. ICASSP, IEEE International Conference on Acoustics, Speech and Signal Processing. 663789, (1192-1196).
7) Lutz et al. (2004). Long-term meditators self-induce high-amplitude gamma synchrony during mental

practice. *Proceedings of the National Academy of Sciences of the United States of America*, 101(46), 16369-16373.

8) Einstein et al. (1935) Can Quantum-Mechanical Descript of Physical Reality Be Considered Complete? Physical Review. 47.

9) Robinson, James. Exegesis on the Soul p 195-196 The Nag Hammadi Library in English

10) Meredith, P; Riesz, J. (2004). Radiative Relaxation Quantum Yields for Synthetic Eumelanin. Photochemistry and Photobiology. 211-216.

11) Solis-Herrera et al. The unexpected capacity of melanin to dissociate the water molecule fills the gap between the life before and after ATP. Biomedical Research 21(2), p 224-226 (2010)

12) Arias-Esparza et al. (2011). The Unexpected Capability of Melanin to Split the Water Molecule and the Alzheimer's Disease. Neuroscience & Medicine, 217-221.

13) Ohwada, K; Taga, N. Vitamin B12, Thiamine, and biotin in lake sagami. Internationale Revue der gesamten Hydrobiologie and Hydrographie, 58(6), 851-871, (1973)

14) Ooi, JH et al. Vitamin D regulates the gut microbiome and protects mice from dextrain sodium sulfate-induced colitis. Journal of Nutrition, 143(10), 1679-1686, (2013)

15) Fernandez, F; Hill, MJ. The production of vitamin k by human gut bacteria. J Med Micriobiol. Volume 10 (1977)
16) Burkholder, P; McVeigh I. Synthesis of Vitamins by Intestinal Bacteria. (1942)
17) Wassef et al. B-Carotene-producing bacteria residing in the intestine provide Vitamin A to mouse tissues in vivo. Journal of Nutrition, 144(5), 608-613, (2014)
18) Herrman et al. Human EEG gamma oscillations in neuropsychiatric disorders. Clinical Neurophysiology, 116(12), 2719-2733.

All biblical quotes are from the NIV, unless stated otherwise:

> Young's Literal Translation (YLT) was often used for bible verses where a literal metaphysical description is required.

> Parenthesis within biblical quotes are notes from the author. Brackets indicate translational disambiguation.

> Special thanks to the greatest bible resource on the web www.biblegateway.com

> Equally special thanks to www.gnosis.org as a free complete online resource for gnostic scripture

Quotes from Plato's Cave Allegory:

> "Plato Book VII of The Republic: The Allegory of the Cave" <webspace.ship.edu/cgboer/platoscave.html>

Quotes from Aristophanes' Theory of Soul Mates:

> http://www.anselm.edu/homepage/dbanach/sym.htm

The L's on Page 22 and 23 are denoting line numbers from The Gospel of Philip translated by Jean-Yves Leloup:

> The Gospel of Philip: Jesus, Mary Magdalene, and the Gnosis of Sacred Union

www.ingramcontent.com/pod-product-compliance
Lightning Source LLC
Chambersburg PA
CBHW031418040426
42444CB00005B/631